Setting The PACE

Stop Reacting to Life
And Start Living It

By
Irawan Hindrawinata

Contents

INTRODUCTION 1

PAUSE 3
   Pause And Be Thankful 6
   Pause And Weigh The Cost 8
   Pause And Be Slow To Anger 10

ASSESS 13
   Assess Your Perspective 15
   Assess Your Priorities 17
   Assess Your Dreams And Set Goals 19
   Assess Your Values And Do The Right Thing 21
   Assess The Value You Add 23

CHOOSE / CONSENT 25
   Choose Your Response 27
   Choose To Forgive And Move On 29
   Choose To Focus On The Present 31
   Choose Who You Want To Become 33

EXECUTE 37
   Execute In Spite Of Fear 38
   Execute Without Excuse 38
   Show Up. On Time. Every Time. 41

KEEPING PACE 43

INTRODUCTION

About a decade ago, the company I was working for sent its leadership team to a team building event. It was good fun and we learned a few valuable lessons on how to work together as a team to create solutions to the issues we were facing. On the bus ride back to the office, I wanted a way to remember the lessons we had learned so that we could apply it to the way we ran our projects. I came up with a simple formula - PACE - that we can use as a guide to identify what our issues were and agree on a solution. I wish I could tell you that I proposed this idea with the "higher ups" and it was adopted into the company's culture and we became a huge success story, but I didn't. I just sat on the idea and kept it to myself.

But it haunted me. I knew it was a great idea and that it would work. In fact, I had applied it to some of my own projects with success. As the years progressed, I kept on thinking about it and the more I thought the more I realized that setting the PACE works in other areas of life as well. It can be a way of life and a guide to how we tackle the everyday problems we faced.

I've always been an addict to personal development. I've read countless books and listened to multiple podcasts from many great minds. The more I learned, and the more I applied to my own life, the more I realized that these life lessons fit naturally into the PACE formula. These are all lessons I want to live my life by and lessons I want my children to learn. The best way to ensure that these lessons don't get lost was to write it all down. And so I did. I write this in the hopes that my children, and anyone else who stumbles across this book can learn from it and set their own PACE in their lives.

Setting a PACE when you are faced with challenge - whether it's a project or an emergency at work or whatever other issue you may be facing in life - means that you Pause instead of mindlessly reacting, Assess the situation and come up with multiple alternatives, Choose/Consent on the solution, and Execute on it. Remembering to apply these steps consistently throughout your life will ensure that you are working towards a well thought out solution, instead of simply reacting to the challenges in life. Setting a PACE gives you (and your team) control over how you will respond.

PAUSE

I was called into a meeting one day and everyone was in a panic over a project that was not going as planned. We were about to lose the client. The client had complained about a process that was being run daily and told the team that they needed to redesign the whole solution. Everyone in the room was frantically trying to come up with a new solution - as was requested by the client. But creating a new solution would take weeks and we didn't have that. I asked the team to take a pause to review what the client actually wanted. Sure he said we needed to create a new solution, but really, all he really wanted was a way to make it so that this one long running process didn't need to be run daily. So we dug deeper and asked why we needed to rerun the process daily. It turned out that it was a work around to some data issue we were seeing. The solution ended up being very simple - fix the incorrect data. This solution took mere hours to code and the client was satisfied.

Everyone in the room had simply been reacting to the angry client's complaint and immediately jumped into action, following his instructions verbatim. What we needed to do was take the time to pause, analyze the issue, and come up with an appropriate response to the request.

We are so quick to automatically react to any situation. The problem is that our automatic reaction may not be the best approach. Our brains are hardwired to try to react as quickly as possible, using whatever past experiences and biases we have (even if they are completely wrong), to get the job done. This is why the first and most important step in any given situation is to first Pause. Before jumping straight into action, take the time to pause and collect yourself. The most important thing to remember in an emergency situation is to not panic and remain calm. You can't effectively help yourself, your family, nor your team members if you are freaking out when a challenge or problem comes up. Pause. Take a deep breath and calm yourself.

Instead of mindlessly executing on the requirements of a project or task at work, pause and make sure you have a clear understanding of the requirements and its intent. Instead of jumping straight into some new and exciting opportunity that will bring you more money, pause and reflect on whether it's aligned with your goals and values. Instead of always wanting to buy the latest and greatest whatever, pause and be thankful for what you've already been blessed with and ask if you really need it. Instead of instantly bursting into a fit of rage when you child breaks the rules or is disrespectful, pause and remind yourself that he/she is really a good kid and has more good qualities than bad. And instead of kicking yourself when you've failed and giving up, pause and see what you can learn from this and move forward.

It's important to note, that this first step is Pause. Not Stop. Once you've paused and collected yourself, it's time to move on to the next step.

Pause And Be Thankful

Kevin seems to have it made. He drives a BMW and lives in a huge house with a garage full of expensive bikes and ATVs. Every time I go over to his house, there is always a new, bigger, TV or some other fancy gadget. His wife and kids all wear the latest name brands and have more toys than they can count. He seems to have it all. But every time we spend time together, he is always complaining. He complains about his car and how he wants to get a better one. He complains that his house just isn't big enough or he needs to add a pool. He complains that his phone is getting old (it's the latest model iPhone) and can't wait for the new one to be released. And he complains that his bosses don't appreciate him and he should be making more money. He has it all, but he is probably the unhappiest person I know.

So many people spend their whole lives chasing "more". No matter how much money they have in the bank, how big their home is, how nice their cars are, and how successful their careers may be, they still want more. These people will never be happy. Sure, they are great at goal setting and achieving, but as soon as they get what they want, it's off to the next thing. They don't even take the time to enjoy what they have.

The secret to true happiness is contentment. Before moving on to the next great thing, pause and be thankful and take the time to enjoy the blessings that you already have. There is always something that you can be thankful for. No matter what it is that you are going through, pause and take the time to see the good in your life.

Make this a habit. Make time, every single day, to pause and find three things that you are thankful for and write it down. Or you can thank God for them in your prayers. Even if you are having a horrible day, there is something that you can be thankful for. Your health. Your home. Your family. Your job. The smile on someone's face as you passed them this morning. There is always something.

Don't get me wrong. Don't think that this is me telling you not to set goals and do your best to succeed in life. By all means, please try your hardest to do all these things. But please remember to always be thankful. Pause and take the time to recognize and enjoy all of God's blessings as you do this.

Pause And Weigh The Cost

Marissa was in tears as she talked to her best friend one evening over coffee. Trying to balance a full-time job and raising her two young kids was getting to be more than she can handle. More than anything, she wants to stay home with the kids and spend as much time as possible with them. But she is unable to, she is drowning in debt. Her husband makes very good money, but they still need her income to make the payments every month and support their lifestyle. She feels trapped.

"The borrower is slave to the lender" - Proverbs 22:7.

You will never enjoy financial nor personal freedom if you are enslaved to debt. Do whatever you can to stay out of debt. With the exception of a mortgage (which you should try to pay off as soon as you can), avoid debt. Your single biggest tool in building wealth is you income. But if that is tied up in paying off your debt, you will not be able to build any wealth.

Don't try to keep up with your friends who have their fancy cars and expensive home. Your friends are likely broke. Don't buy anything you can't afford to pay for in full. A car drives so much better when it's not dragging along a payment. So, before you sign yourself into slavery to get the latest and greatest thing that you probably don't need anyways, pause and understand its true cost.

Getting into debt can cost you your personal freedom to chase your dreams and focus on your priorities. Being heavily in debt means you will have huge bills to pay at the end of every month. You are stuck with the responsibility of having to make the income to pay this. If you don't like your job, or if there is a dream you want to chase, or if you decide that you want to stay home with your kids, you won't be able to. The debt collectors don't care about your dreams nor the well-being of your children. They only care about the money you owe them.

True personal and financial freedom comes from living a life of gratitude and having the discipline to delay gratification and saving up for the things you want. Don't fall for the lie that debt is a tool you can leverage. Regardless of what the numbers tell you, personal finance is more about your behavior than anything else.

Pause And Be Slow To Anger

I once was told that my son was sent out of his class along with a couple of his friends to spend the next hour or so doing nothing but sharpen pencils. What?!? Why was he sent out for so long? Why can't his teacher sharpen her own pencils for the class? He is such a gifted student, why is he wasting his time doing this instead of learning more? I should switch the class he's in. I need to write to the principal. I need to confront his teacher about this... I was ready for battle. But instead, I paused and gathered more information. Turns out the class was taking a test and he and his friends had finished early. Usually, he would pull out his book and read while the rest of the class continued with their test, but this day he had forgotten it. He also had noticed that the teacher had a bunch of pencils donated to her by other parents and that they were unsharpened. He thought it would be nice to sharpen them for the class so they would be ready to use should anyone needed them. So he asked his teacher if he could help out and his teacher agreed. It wasn't a punishment. His talents weren't being wasted. He was simply doing a good deed for his teacher and fellow classmates. I'm glad I paused instead of jumping straight into action and doing something I would have regretted.

It's so easy for us to jump into action or a fit of rage over the slightest trespass. But our first instinct is not always the correct path to take. Someone cuts you off on your way to work. Your first instinct might be that this person is a jerk who doesn't care about anyone but himself and you want to give him a piece of your mind. But really, what good is this? Will it undo the fact that he cut you off? Is he really a jerk? Or could he have just not seen you? Pause, take a breath, and realize that there are more factors involved and many different paths that you can choose to take.

ASSESS

Simply taking the time to pause and gather yourself is a great first step. But you have to also take the next step and Assess the issue at hand. Identify what the problem is, what the end goal should look like, and come up with some options on how you can reach your goals.

First off, is there really a problem? Does it actually need to be fixed? Is it worth your time and energy? Or is there something better you should be doing? Or perhaps there really isn't a problem and you've just been looking at it from the wrong perspective.

Once you've identified that there is a problem and what the problem is, your next step is to identify what the end should look like - not what to do about it. Dale Carnegie says that one of the habits of highly effective people is that they "start with the end in mind." If you don't know what you are aiming for, then how do you know if you've hit the target? You have to be clear on where you want to go before charting out which path on the map you want to take.

With the end goal in mind, try to come up with a few options on how to achieve that goal. Oftentimes your first option is simply what you are most comfortable doing or what someone else has told you to do. But it might not be the right path to take. There may be better alternatives that will yield better results in the long run. Take the time to come up with a few options here.

Be careful... people can get stuck in this step. There may be so many variables in play that people get stuck trying to account for everything that may (or may not) happen. Don't let this happen to you. Come up with a few options and move on. You can (and should) always pause again and reassess once you get moving.

Assess Your Perspective

"How you see the problem IS the problem" - Dale Carnegie

Jason was unhappy with where he was in life - especially with regards to his job. He was good at what he did and was making very good money, but he was not passionate about it. His dream is to go around the world with his mountain bike and take on all the toughest trails. But, how could he? He has bills to pay and a family to take care of. How would he ever be able to make enough to do all that on a mountain bike? He's not particularly great at mountain biking, so he can't really turn pro. Maybe he can start a YouTube channel that features his adventures. But it would take forever, if at all, to make any real money doing that. He's stuck in his job daydreaming all day about winning the lottery so that he may one day be able to chase his dreams.

Jason and I go out on hikes a couple times a month so we can catch up and enjoy the trails in our area. On one of these hikes, he shared with me his frustrations. I asked how he got into mountain biking in the first place. He said his co-worker invited him to go out with him once a few years ago and he was hooked. I asked how much he spent on his bike (I was interested and wanted to know a ballpark figure of how much it took to start mountain biking). He said about $3500 but it was ok since he had his finances in order and he was able to work it into his budget. I asked how often he biked and how much time it took to go out on the trails. He said it takes a few hours at least and he's able to go out a few times a month. And since his work schedule is pretty flexible, he's able to do so without sacrificing time with his family.

At this point, I was confused. It seemed to me that if it weren't for his job - the thing he's complaining about - he wouldn't have been able to mountain bike at all. It introduced him to the sport. It paid for the equipment. And it gave him the time to go out and enjoy biking without spending any time away from his family. His job wasn't a problem to be solved, it was a blessing to be realized. I shared my thoughts with him and he agreed. He didn't need to change anything about his job. He just needed to change his perspective. He could continue to work hard and be successful in the office *and* enjoy going out on the trails and have an adventure.

If you have an issue that you've been struggling with for some time now, pause and assess the situation. Is there really a problem here to be solved? Sometimes there isn't and that the only real problem is your perspective.

Assess Your Priorities

We are all very busy. There are so many things that vie for our attention; our kids, our spouses, our dreams, our bosses, our teammates. The list goes on and on. Some of these things are urgent - they want your attention and want it now - some are not. Some are important - they increase your health, your wealth, your success, and your relationships - some are not. The trick is being able to assess which is which and focus your best energies on the things that are important.

The things that are urgent and important are easy to spot. You really don't need to try very hard to identify them. They usually find you. And dedicating your time and energy on these are fairly automatic.

The things that are not important - urgent or not - are your biggest time and energy vampires. You need to exercise your willpower to avoid these. I'm talking about things like friends calling you to give you the latest gossip when you are trying to work; the latest episode of some inane reality TV show everyone is telling you about; and the video game all your friends are playing and you just can't get enough of. None of these things are going to move you forward to meeting your goals. Don't waste any more time on these if you still have more important things to do.

The things that you need to focus on for your success are the important but not urgent. These are things like exercise, spending quality time with your family, reading to increase your knowledge and personal growth, writing that book you've always wanted to write, and taking the time to meditate and pray. None of these scream for your attention right now, but if you don't make them a priority, they can easily move over to the urgent category. Before you know it, you'll be served divorce papers, or your neglected body will suddenly give out on you. So, before you do anything else, and before other urgent things try to distract you, spend time to focus on the important.

Your time, energy, focus and willpower are limited. As the day wears on, these resources are drained and they will not be recharged until you've gone to sleep. This is why you need to focus on important things first. Make it a habit to wake up a bit earlier every day and devote this time to doing the important things that are not screaming for your attention. It may be hard at first, but the benefits you'll get from doing this will be huge. If you practice this every single day, it will be easier to do. Once something becomes a habit, you won't need to exert much effort or willpower to do them, leaving you with more for the rest of your day. So do the things that matter to you, your dreams, your life, your family, and your career first.

Assess Your Dreams And Set Goals

In order to move forward in life, you should always be setting goals. Goals point you in the direction you should be moving. More importantly, it keeps you moving in that direction instead of just aimlessly roaming about. You may not know how to get there yet, nor what challenges you'll face, but by setting a goal, you will know where you are going and when you've arrived. Zig Ziglar says that "if you aim at nothing, you will hit it every time."

Sean Stephenson says that the secret to your emotional well-being is to always have goals. Not necessarily to always achieve your goals, but just to have goals. You should always try to meet them, of course, but the true benefit of having a goal is that it keeps you focused on the present - with an eye to the future - instead of lamenting over the past. You can't change the past, but you can let it go and choose how you will live the rest of your life. Goals will help you do this.

Jim Rohn says that the main benefit of setting goals and going after them is not reaching them, but rather becoming the person who can reach them. Want to be physically fit? Become someone who is fit. Watch what you eat. Exercise daily. Want to be a millionaire? Become someone who has a million-dollar net worth. Save more than you make. Work hard. Work smart. Invest and take smart risks.

I suggest you set goals for each area of your life - your health, your family, your career, your friendships, and your wealth. To start, set smaller goals so you can gain momentum and set progressively larger goals. As I write this, my goal for this book is to finish one section every week day. It doesn't have to be perfect; it just has to be done. My overarching goal is to have this book published, but before that, I'm starting small. My original goal was to have one section done a week (even smaller), but once I started doing it, it gave me such encouragement that I couldn't wait to write more each day, so I've shifted it to a section a day. There's nothing wrong with shifting your goals around to meet your current circumstances. It's not necessarily about achieving your goals, it's about the process of setting goals and moving forward.

Goals help tell you where you are and where you are going. They keep your eyes forward and give you the motivation to keep moving. Set some today. Write them down and look at them a few times a day.

Assess Your Values And Do The Right Thing

I wanted to try out mountain biking one day so I started doing some research on which bike I should buy. I didn't know how much I would enjoy it, so I didn't want to invest too much money. I figured I would invest maybe $500 into a new bike, and if I really liked it, I would invest more into a better bike. So, I went to a bike shop to get some help. I explained my situation to the guy who greeted me and he proceeded to show me the latest and greatest bike that was more than twice my price range. When I explained to him again that I didn't want to spend so much, he showed me another bike that was still a few hundred dollars above the range I gave him. Then he proceeded to tell me the benefits of the first bike he showed me. Instead of taking the time to assess my needs, he was trying to make the perfect sale. What he got was a disgruntled customer who will never go back to that shop again.

You don't have to be perfect to succeed in life. The most successful people are the ones that have failed the most times, but have remained committed to achieving their goals. They choose to learn from their mistakes and move forward. They also let their values guide them instead of their greed. When given the choice to serve others or do what will benefit them the most, they will choose to serve and do the right thing. The more people you serve the more successful you will become. Don't ever try to sell someone something they don't need. Take the time to listen to their needs, properly assess the situation, and serve them accordingly. You will create customers who are loyal and will come back for more.

Assess The Value You Add

I tried flipping real estate a few times with some success. The real estate agent I had at the time, Rick, was awesome. He was quick to answer any questions I had. He listened to my needs and never wasted my time with properties that were way beyond the requirements I had given him. But what made me use him as my agent over and over again was what he did on the first property I worked on. It was a good property that only needed a minor face lift. When we did the walk through to see what needed to be done, he suggested some fresh tiling around the fireplace and volunteered to do the job himself! I couldn't believe it. He was a busy agent with plenty of other clients, but instead of simply closing the deal on this property and moving on to the next client, he saw a need and took the time to fill it.

Regardless of where your career may take you and what position you hold, remember - you are ultimately in a customer service role. Always be asking the question, "How can I better serve others?" No matter what your job title is, always try to provide more value than what you are paid to do. This is one of the shortest ways I know of to move forward in your career. I don't mean kill yourself working all day and all night. You can add value by working smarter and looking for opportunities to streamline how you and/or your team does the job. If you are able to do what you are paid for in less time, this will leave you more time to do more and add value. Don't bother running around chasing recognition. Work smart, work hard, and let your work do the talking for you.

The more people you serve, the more value you add. If you see a teammate struggling, help them out. You don't have to do their job for them, but you can encourage, lend a hand, guide, or coach them. The more you do this, the more value you add to yourself and your team. Your pay raise will become effective when you are. Don't ask for promotion or a raise before you've proven yourself. Add value first, so it becomes impossible for anyone to say no to your request. If you serve enough people and add more value than what you are paid to do, success will follow.

CHOOSE / CONSENT

Once you have assessed the issue at hand and have come up with a couple of alternative solutions, the next step is to Choose which path you will take. The most important lesson to remember here is that you always have a choice. And that the responsibility to choose is yours and yours alone. If you are in a team environment (whether it's a project team, your family, or you and your spouse), you will need to gain Consensus from everyone involved before you move forward. Everyone on the team will need to either agree to the solution or at least be comfortable with moving forward without getting in the way. If anyone is uncomfortable, or disagrees with the solution, the team needs to discuss what their concerns are and address it. Sometimes this is just a matter of giving more information, other times it means coming up with a different alternative. In either case, take the time to gain consensus from all involved before moving forward. Nothing is more toxic to a project than a team member who is not on board with the solution. They will drag you down like an anchor.

James was a hard worker and very intelligent. We worked together on a very complicated project. It took us many months of endlessly unproductive meetings just to gather the requirements. The reason these meetings would drag and be so unproductive was that James would continually challenge every decision we tried to make. I took him aside one day after an extremely frustrating session and asked why he was being so difficult. Turns out, he was uncomfortable with what we were trying to do and was unclear why we were doing it. Once it was clear to him what we were trying to do and how it benefits the client, he was on fire. Not only was he one of the most productive members of the team, but he came up with some very innovative solutions that made the project a bigger success than anyone imagined it could be.

Choose Your Response

Regardless of what happens around you and whose fault it is. You are responsible for how you will respond. There is no point in trying to figure out whose fault something is, the problem will still be there. It is a far better use of your time to figure out what you are going to do about it. What can you do to make this better? How are you going to respond? The choice is yours.

You can't control others and you can't change who they are. The only person you really have any control over is you. The only person who can change who you are and control how you behave is you. You can't control how others will treat you. But you can control how you respond to them. You can choose to respond with kindness. You can choose to respond with hate. You can choose to respond with tears. Or you can choose to walk away. The point is that you have the power to choose.

No matter where you find yourself in life. You have the responsibility of choosing what happens next. Will you stay put? Or will you choose a new goal and take the next steps towards that goal? Will you sit around moping about your situation, whining about it to anyone who will listen? Or will you make the choice to change the situation and make the most of the life God has given you and be grateful for all that you have? It's your choice. It's your responsibility to make that choice. If you want a better life, you have to choose to change and put in the hard work. Life gives opportunities to those who deserve it. The crop won't come in until you've chosen to sow the seeds and diligently work the soil. Stop making excuses and blaming others for your situation. Choose to take responsibility for your life and make a change.

Choose To Forgive And Move On

"No one can hurt you without your permission." - Eleanor Roosevelt

Sometimes you will come across people whom you will not get along with. There will always be haters and critics. Especially if you are on your way to becoming successful in life. That's ok. Let them hate. You won't be able to control what people say or do, but you can control how you respond to their hate. You get to choose whether or not their words will generate tears and hatred (which is what they really want), or love, kindness, or no response at all.

When you respond to hateful words with love and kindness, you take away their power and take back control of your life. Things people say will sting the moment they say them - I'm not going to pretend they won't - but you have the choice whether or not you will let the hurt get deep into your heart and poison your soul.

Forgive and move on. Remember, forgiveness is all about you. It's about taking control of your mind and spirit and letting go of the hurt and hatred. Forgiveness is not the same as reconciling. You don't have to go back for more, but you do have to let it go and let your heart heal. It may seem impossible sometimes, but it's actually pretty simple. You just have to say the words, "I choose to let this go and take back control of my life." You don't even have to to say it to anyone in particular. You just have to say it to yourself - out loud is even better - and repeat it every time the negative feelings come back.

No one has the power to make you feel anything unless you let them. Believe it or not, you are the source of all your emotions - not some external event. Hal Elrod says that all negative emotion comes from your rejection of reality. All positive emotions start from your acceptance of reality and choosing to move forward. You have the power to choose. Don't give this power away.

Choose To Focus On The Present

No matter where you are and how you got there, your focus needs to be on the present. Don't linger on the past. There is nothing you can do to change what has already happened. There is no point in constantly replaying whatever events have happened in the past over and over again. It's in the past. You can't change it and you can't get back to it. But you do have the power to choose to focus on what is going on around you today. You have the choice to be thankful for where you are and what you've been blessed with. You have a choice to make a difference in your or someone else's life. You have the power to change the future.

Stay in the present so you can make a better tomorrow. But don't lose focus on the present and start worrying about the future. Worry does absolutely nothing for you but stress you out. Just like the fact that you can't change the past. You can't control what may or may not happen in the future. You can be smart and prepare for it. You can do what you can to point yourself in the direction you want your life to go, but tomorrow is never guaranteed for anyone. So don't spend so much time on the *what if's* and enjoy and work on the *what is*.

You should learn from the past and you should definitely be setting goals for the future. But don't let yourself lose focus on the present. The present - where you are now - is the only thing you have any control over. Don't waste any more of your energy and attention on anything else.

Choose Who You Want To Become

Bob Ross is famous for teaching people how to paint beautiful landscapes. He is equally famous for his mellow soft-spoken demeanor. In fact, I've even heard of people downloading episodes of his show, "The Joy of Painting," just so they can listen to it while they sleep. But he wasn't always this way. In fact, he used to make a living screaming at people and barking out orders as a Master Sergeant in the Air Force. When he left the military, he chose to make a change and promised to never raise his voice again.

You too have the power to choose who you want to be. You don't have to be stuck being the person you've become. Things may have happened in the past that have made you an angry or bitter person, but that does not mean that that is who you have to be for the rest of your life. You have the choice to change who you are. You have the power to be the type of person you want to be.

Let go of the past, forgive those who have hurt you. There is nothing you can do to change what has already happened. But you can choose to let it go and focus on the present instead of dwelling in the past. Remember, forgiveness is not about the other person. It's about you. It's about taking the power back and making a choice to move on. If you continue to be angry and filled with hatred, you are giving away your power to choose your attitude to the other person. So, let go, forgive, and choose to move forward.

Start small. If you want to be a happier person, start by smiling more. If you want to get healthier, get up and go for a walk. If you want to be a better husband, wife, father, or mother, ask how the other person is doing and listen. Changing who you are doesn't have to be a huge complicated thing. Keep it simple by simply choosing something to do differently and doing it. No matter how long or hard this next journey is going to be, it starts with a single step. You don't have to completely overhaul your whole life at once. You just have to make a choice and start.

Choose The Path Of Least Regret

My kids all have late birthdays. This meant that we had the option of choosing whether or not we wanted to start them in Kindergarten when they were still 4 years old or give them another year. We laid out our options; keep them in preschool for another year - which would cost $5000 each, or send them off to Kindergarten as soon as they were allowed to. It would be nice to save that money, but we knew that giving them an extra year would make sure they had the time to mature so that it would be easier for them to learn. We could take the money and invest it into their college fund and let it grow for 12 years, or we could invest the time and money into giving our kids the advantage of being the older kid in class. We chose to analyze this from a different angle. Which path would we regret the least? If we gave them another year of preschool, we would be losing out on the money. I can always just make more money later. But if we sent them off to Kindergarten early, there's a chance they might not be ready and end up getting held back in 3rd or 4th grade - there is nothing we can do to reverse that. We can't get that time back. Sending them off early could lead to the most regret, so we gave each of our kids that extra year. And so far, it's been paying off tremendously.

If you are having trouble choosing which course of action to take, try looking into the future to see which action would lead to the least regret. Sometimes, you will come across a choice where the rewards are fairly even, but the consequences are vastly different. Even if one option may yield a greater reward, or it seems like the easier path to take, it may end in a result that you can't undo and you'll regret it for the rest of your life.

I want to be clear here. I'm not suggesting that you choose the path of least risk. I'm suggesting you choose the path of least regret. Choosing the safest route, like not chasing your dreams, may be safe, but will oftentimes lead to the most regret. Remember, even if things go wrong, you can learn something from it and use what you've learned as you go after your next adventure.

Choosing the path of least regret means you need to answer these two questions, weigh out the answers, and make a choice: 1) Which path, if things go wrong, will lead to the most regret? Some consequences you just can't undo or get back no matter how hard you work at it. 2) Which path, if not taken, will lead to the most regret? The safety and comfort of one path may not outweigh the resentment and regret you may feel for not taking a chance and daring to succeed.

EXECUTE

Now that you have a plan of action in place, it's time to Execute on it. Take action and do what you have chosen to do and work as hard and as smart as you can at it. Nothing leads to more regret than knowing what you should be doing, but not doing it.

Many of us are personal development junkies. We read and read and read. We listen to endless hours of podcasts by all the great minds. But we don't do anything about it. I spent a decade dreaming to someday write this book so I can perhaps help just one other person with it. But I never took action. I never executed on the dream. I wasted so much time. Don't let that happen to you. Take action! Push fear aside, don't give up, and keep showing up and making progress.

Execute In Spite Of Fear

The most successful people are not the ones that always succeed, but rather are the ones that take the most shots and learned from all their failures. Don't fear failure. A failure is only a failure if you don't pick yourself up, learn from your mistakes, and try again. You will never succeed at anything unless you take some action. It doesn't have to be perfectly planned, but once you have chosen what the next move is that will point you in the right direction to reach your goal, get moving. Even if the results are not what you expected, you can learn and adjust. But if you are paralyzed with fear and don't take the next step, then nothing will get accomplished.

Fear is very tricky. It plays both sides of the failure coin. It told me that I can't write this book because I don't have enough content for a book. And it told me that there is so much I want to share that I can't possibly put it all down into words. It told me that I should have started writing a long time ago, it's too late. And it told me that I can't possibly start now, I don't have enough time. Don't let fear trick you any longer. You have to act.

If failure is what you still fear most, think of it this way. You will miss 100% of the shots you don't take. Inaction is the surest way to fail at anything. So let go of your fears and insecurities and just try. You will never know if you can do something unless you give it a shot. Life is just too short to live in fear. Get moving!

Execute Without Excuse

"You can make progress or you can make excuses" - Chris Hogan

The only reason you have for not working on your personal development is that you have not chosen to do so. Regardless of where you find yourself and who has caused you pain, you have the power to choose whether that will be your excuse for not growing or if you will take that step to reach your goals.

What are your goals and what actions are you taking to get you closer to meeting your goals? You have to take that first step towards your goals, no matter how big they are, in order to reach them. No matter how long the journey is, it starts with a single small step. Even if this step is not in the right direction, you can always course correct. But if you don't take that first step because you are afraid to fail, then this is just another excuse and you will never make any progress.

Keep moving forward. Once you've taken that first step, the next one will be easier and so will the next one after that. Some people use motivation as an excuse for not taking action. They just don't feel motivated enough. But really, it's the other way around. You have to make the choice to take action and once you've done so, that action will give you the motivation and momentum to take the next action.

Show Up. On Time. Every Time.

Show up. Show up to your classes. Show up at work. Show up to your practice. Show up to your kids' practice. Show up for dinner. Just show up. Half of the effort to any endeavor is showing up. If you don't do that, then you will fail every time. But just showing up is not enough. You have to make a real effort to show up on time, every time.

Time is a precious resource. It's the only thing that you can't get more of once it's gone. So you have to respect it. And you have to respect everyone else's time. That's why I'm such a stickler when it comes to showing up to everything on time. When you are late to something, you are making the statement that whatever it is, it is not that important to you. When you make someone wait, you are stating that your time is more important than theirs. Even when no one else is waiting, show up on time. By doing so, you are making a statement to yourself that this is important and you are going to give it the attention and respect it deserves.

Time is the currency of the heart. Whatever you spend the most of your waking hours on is where your heart truly lies. If family is your number one priority, then you need to show up for dinner on time, every time, so you can share a meal and talk about the day with them. Show up to your kids' practices and games so you can support and encourage them. Show up and be there for your spouse and children. Your very presence shows them that you care.

The same principle applies to work and school. Show up on time, every time. With the exception of the sick or vacation days, you need to show yourself and others that you take your career/education seriously and want to add value and grow.

Your health is no exception to this. I don't care what form of exercise you do, but you've got to show up. Prove to yourself that you matter by showing up to your workout on time, every time. Like I've said before, showing up is half the battle. Even if you don't feel like it, just show up. Once you are there, you are more likely to go ahead and put the work in.

Just showing up is not enough, though. You've actually got to be present when you are there. If you're in class, pay attention. If you are at work, work. If you are at home with the family or out on a date, put your phone down and pay attention. I'm very guilty of this myself and am working on that.

Time flies by so very quickly and some opportunities only come once in a lifetime. If you are not there to take advantage of it, if you've failed to show up, you'll miss out on some of the most important things that life has to offer. Show up.

KEEPING PACE

As you progress through to your goals, you have to check your PACE regularly. As you are executing your solution, take the time to Pause what you are doing, Assess that your goals are still in line with your values, Choose any necessary adjustments, and Execute on the plan.

I've learned that how you do anything is how you do everything. Setting a PACE is an effective way to work through life's challenges and problems. But you can also set a PACE to your daily life. In the mornings, before the rush of the day starts, Pause and take some time to meditate and focus on a few things you are grateful for. Assess what your goals are for the day and plan out what you can do to accomplish those goals. Choose which paths you will take and Execute on it.

As the day progresses, take some time to Pause before reacting to a challenge or problem. Assess what you are going to do to solve these problems. Come up with at least one other alternative. Choose which one is best, making sure you have the Consent of any other teammates, and Execute the plan.

In the evening, before you turn in for the night, Pause and reflect on the day. Assess what lessons you've learned, especially from any "failures". Choose love and gratitude over any other emotion, and Execute these choices over any fear and regret.

Keep setting the PACE of your own life. Stop reacting to everything that life throws at you and start living it.

www.ingramcontent.com/pod-product-compliance
Lightning Source LLC
Chambersburg PA
CBHW070859220526
45466CB00005B/2044